NIKON Z9
POCKET GUIDE

TABLE OF CONTENTS

01 PRE-SHOOT CHECKLIST

Check these settings before you head out with your camera!

SETTING	MY PREFERRED SETTING
☑ Shooting Mode	....
☑ White Balance Setting	....
☑ ISO Setting	....
☑ Focus Mode	....
☑ AF-Area Mode	....
☑ Release Mode	....
☑ Metering Mode	....
☑ Bracketing: On/Off	....
☑ File Format: JPEG, RAW, or RAW+JPEG	....
☑ Highlight Warning: On/Off	....
☑ Vibration Reduction: On/Off/Sport	....
☑ Picture Control	....
☑ Flash Mode	....
☑ Battery Fully Charged and In Camera	....
☑ Memory Card(s) Formatted and In Camera	....

02 BUTTONS, DIALS, AND SCREENS

CAMERA BODY TOP

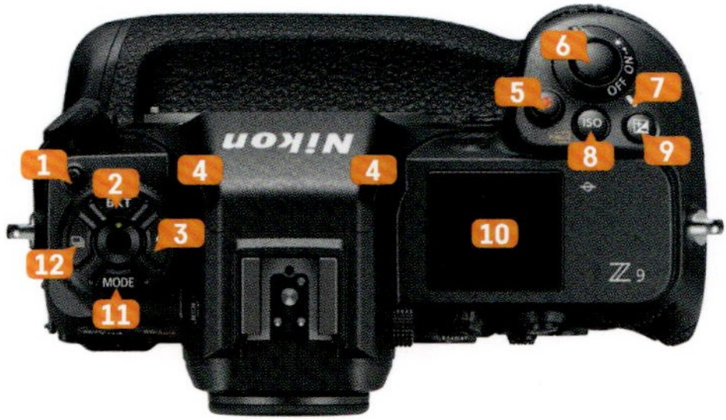

1. **Release Mode Dial Lock Release:** Press to unlock the Release Mode Dial. (See Release Mode Dial on page XX.)
2. **BKT Button:** Use with the Main Command Dial and Sub-Command Dial to set the number of frames and the change in between them when bracketing.
3. **Flash Button:** Press button and rotate Main Command Dial to set flash mode.
4. **Stereo Microphones:** Used to record audio when shooting video.
5. **Video Record Button:** Start and stop video recording when camera is set to video mode.

6. **Shutter Release Button:** Press halfway down to activate autofocus and all the way down to take photo.

7. **On / Off Switch:** Turn camera on and off.

8. **ISO Button:** Press button and rotate Main Command Dial to adjust ISO.

9. **Exposure Compensation Button:** Press button and rotate Main Command Dial to adjust exposure compensation.

10. **Control Panel:** Shows current camera settings.

11. **Mode Button:** Press button and rotate Main Command Dial to change shooting mode between P (Programmed Auto), A (Aperture Priority), S (Shutter Speed Priority), and M (Manual).

12. **Release Mode Button:** Use with Main Command Dial to change release mode when the Release Mode Dial is set to .

CAMERA BODY BACK

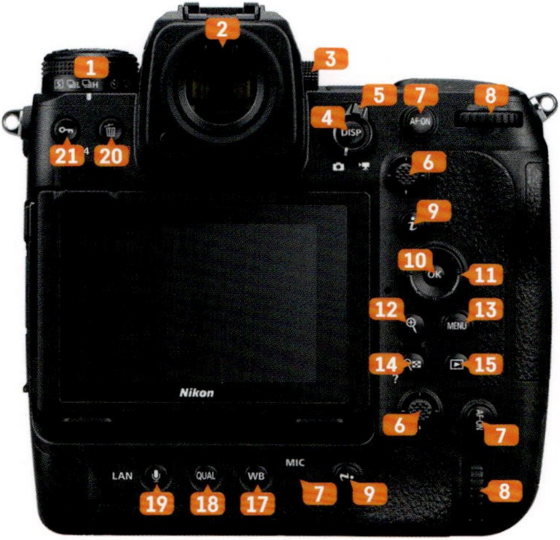

1. **Release Mode Dial:** Rotate to select the release mode. Must press the Release Mode Dial Lock Release first.
2. **Eye Sensor:** Switches display from monitor to viewfinder when eye is at viewfinder.
3. **Diopter Adjustment:** Adjust diopter of viewfinder.
4. **DISP Button:** Cycle through display screens.
5. **Photo/Video Selector:** Switch between photo and video modes.

6. **Sub-Selector:** Use as a joystick to select focus point. Press and hold to lock focus and exposure.
7. **AF-ON Button:** Press to engage autofocus.
8. **Main Command Dial:** Use to adjust camera settings.
9. **𝒾 Button:** Opens contextual menu depending on camera mode.
10. **OK Button:** Select current option.
11. **Multi Selector:** Navigate menus or select AF point.
12. **Magnify Button:** Zoom in on current image shown on LCD.
13. **Menu Button:** Open and close camera menu system.
14. **Zoom Out Button:** Zoom out on current image shown on LCD.
15. **Playback Button:** Show last image taken on LCD.
16. **Microphone for Voice Memos:** Used to record voice memos.
17. **White Balance Button:** Use with Main Command Dial to set white balance.
18. **Qual Button:** Use with Main Command Dial to set image quality.
19. **Microphone Button:** Press to record voice memo. Only one voice memo per image.
20. **Trash:** Delete current image on LCD.
21. **Protect / Fn4 Button:** Press during playback to protect current image; or press button and rotate Main Command Dial to set Picture Controls.

CAMERA BODY FRONT

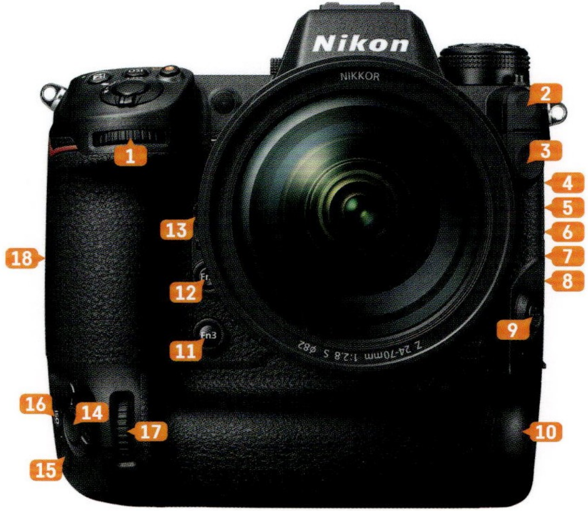

1. **Sub-Command Dial:** Use to adjust camera settings.
2. **Flash Sync Terminal (under cover):** Connect flash sync cable.
3. **10-Pin Remote Terminal (under cover):** Connect 10-pin remote.
4. **Ethernet Connector (under cover on side):** Connect ethernet cable.
5. **External Microphone Connector (under cover on side):** Connect external microphones.

6. **Headphone Connector (under cover on side):** Connect external headphones.

7. **HDMI Connector (under cover on side):** Connect HDMI cable.

8. **USB Connector (under cover on side):** Connect USB cable.

9. **Focus Mode Button:** Use with Main Command Dial to change focus mode.

10. **Battery Chamber Cover:** Battery goes in here.

11. **Fn3 Button:** Programmable button set to Live View Info Display Off as default.

12. **Fn2 Button:** Programmable button set to Choose Image Area as default.

13. **Fn1 Button:** Programmable button set to Shooting Menu Bank as default.

14. **Shutter Release Button and Shutter Release Lock (for vertical shooting):** Press halfway down to activate autofocus and all the way down to take photo. Can be locked so it doesn't inadvertently get pressed when not in use.

15. **Fn Button (for vertical shooting):** Programmable function button set to Exposure Compensation as default.

16. **ISO Button (for vertical shooting):** Press and rotate Main Command Dial to adjust ISO.

17. **Sub-Command Dial (for vertical shooting):** Use to adjust camera settings.

18. **Memory Card Slots (under cover on side):** Memory cards go in here.

VIEWFINDER DISPLAY (PHOTO)

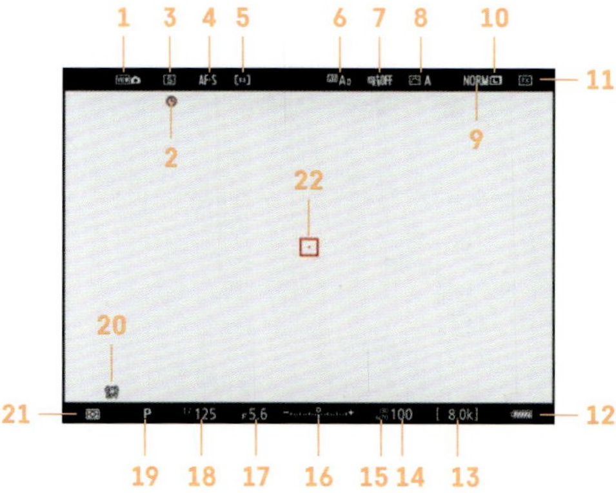

1. **View Mode:** Shows the current view mode.
2. **Clock Not Set Indicator:** When flashing, the date and time need to be set. Setup Menu > Time zone and date > Date and time.
3. **Release Mode:** Shows current release mode.
4. **Focus Mode:** Shows current focus mode.
5. **AF-Area Mode:** Shows current AF-area mode.
6. **White Balance:** Shows current WB setting.
7. **Active D-Lighting:** Displays the Active D-Lighting status.
8. **Picture Control:** Displays current Picture Control.
9. **Image Quality:** Shows the current image quality: RAW, RAW+JPEG, or JPEG.
10. **Image Size:** Shows current image size.

11. **Image Area:** Shows the current image area: FX for full frame or DX for cropped sensor.

12. **Battery Indicator:** Displays the amount of battery power remaining.

13. **Number of Exposures Remaining:** Shows the number of photos that can still be taken based on the current settings and the space available on the memory card.

14. **ISO Sensitivity:** Shows current ISO.

15. **ISO / Auto ISO Sensitivity Indicator:** Shows if Auto ISO is enabled.

16. **Exposure / Exposure Compensation Indicator:** Shows current exposure and if any exposure compensation is applied.

17. **Aperture:** Shows current aperture.

18. **Shutter Speed:** Shows current shutter speed.

19. **Shooting Mode:** Shows current shooting mode P, A, S, M.

20. **Vibration Reduction Indicator:** Shows if VR is turned on.

21. **Metering Mode:** Shows current metering mode.

22. **Focus Point:** Shows selected focus point(s).

VIEWFINDER DISPLAY (MOVIE)

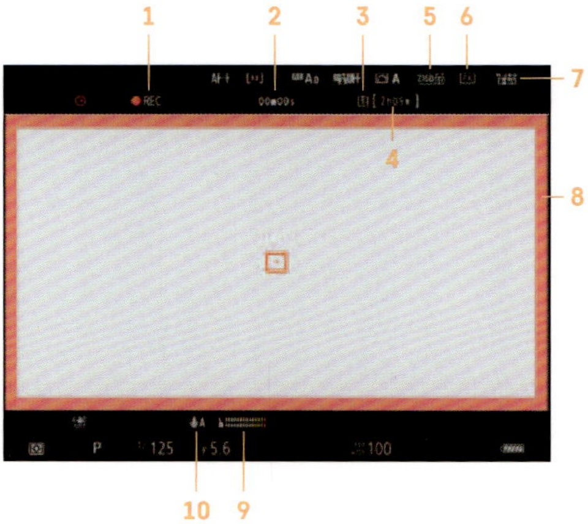

1. **Recording Indicator / Recording Disabled:** Shows when movies are being recorded; shows when movies cannot be recorded.
2. **Video Recording Time:** Shows the amount of time the current video has been recording.
3. **Destination:** Shows which card slot video is being saved to.
4. **Time Remaining:** Shows the amount of time remaining until memory card is full based on the current settings.
5. **Frame Size / Frame Rate:** Shows current frame size / frame rate.
6. **Image Area:** Shows current image area: FX or DX.
7. **Video File Type:** Shows the current video file type.

8. **Recording Indicator:** A red border around the viewfinder activates when camera is recording video.

9. **Sound Level:** Shows current sound levels.

10. **Microphone Sensitivity:** Shows current microphone sensitivity settings.

MONITOR DISPLAY (PHOTO)

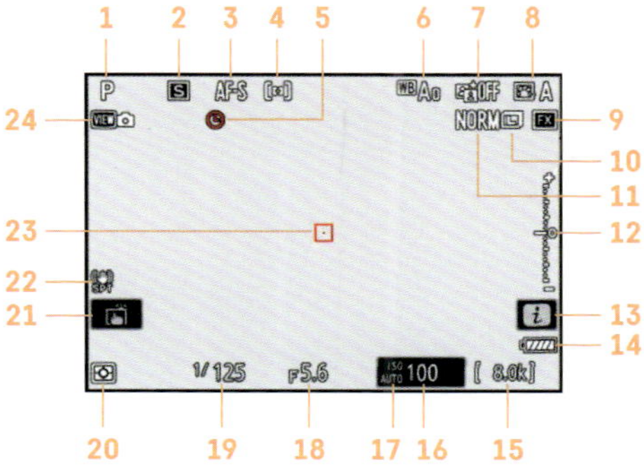

1. **Shooting Mode:** Shows current shooting mode P, A, S, M.
2. **Release Mode:** Shows current release mode.
3. **Focus Mode:** Shows current focus mode.
4. **AF-Area Mode:** Shows current AF-area mode.
5. **Clock Not Set Indicator:** When flashing, the date and time need to be set. Setup Menu > Time zone and date > Date and time.
6. **White Balance:** Shows current WB setting.

7. **Active D-Lighting:** Displays the Active D-Lighting status.
8. **Picture Control:** Displays current Picture Control.
9. **Image Area:** Shows the current image area: FX for full frame or DX for cropped sensor.
10. **Image Size:** Shows current image size.
11. **Image Quality:** Shows the current image quality: RAW, RAW+JPEG, or JPEG.
12. **Exposure / Exposure Compensation Indicator:** Shows current exposure and if any exposure compensation is applied.
13. *i* **Icon:** Tap the *i* icon to open the *i* Menu.
14. **Battery Indicator:** Displays the amount of battery power remaining.
15. **Number of Exposures Remaining:** Shows the number of photos that can still be taken based on the current settings and the space available on the memory card.
16. **ISO Sensitivity:** Shows current ISO.
17. **ISO / Auto ISO Sensitivity Indicator:** Shows if Auto ISO is enabled.
18. **Aperture:** Shows current aperture.
19. **Shutter Speed:** Shows current shutter speed.
20. **Metering Mode:** Shows current metering mode.
21. **Touch Shooting:** Shows if touch shooting is enabled.
22. **Vibration Reduction:** Shows if VR is turned on.
23. **Focus Point:** Shows selected focus point(s).
24. **View Mode:** Shows the current view mode.

MONITOR DISPLAY (MOVIE)

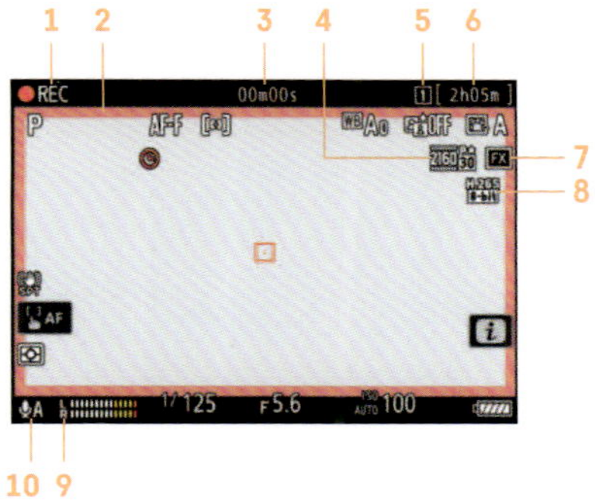

1. Recording Indicator / Recording Disabled: Shows when movies are being recorded; shows when movies cannot be recorded.

2. Recording Indicator: A red border around the display activates when camera is recording video.

3. Video Recording Time: Shows the amount of time the current video has been recording.

4. Frame Size / Frame Rate: Shows current frame size / frame rate.

5. Destination: Shows which card slot video is being saved to.

6. Time Remaining: Shows the amount of time remaining until memory card is full based on the current settings.

7. Image Area: Shows current image area: FX or DX.

8. Video File Type: Shows the current video file type.

9. Sound Level: Shows current sound levels.

10. Microphone Sensitivity: Shows current microphone sensitivity settings.

CONTROL PANEL

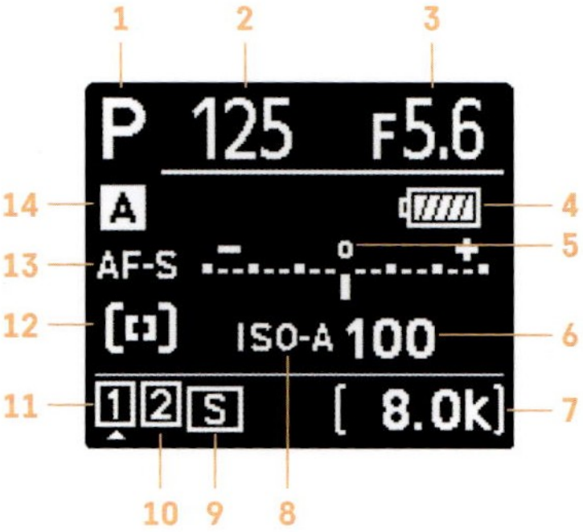

1. **Shooting Mode:** Shows current shooting mode P, A, S, M.
2. **Shutter Speed:** Shows current shutter speed.
3. **Aperture:** Shows current aperture.
4. **Battery Indicator:** Displays the amount of battery power remaining.
5. **Exposure Indicator:** Shows effect of current settings on the exposure.
6. **ISO:** Shows current ISO.
7. **Number of Exposures Remaining / Available Recording Time:** Shows the number of images that can still be taken using current settings; shows the amount of video footage that can still be recorded using current settings.
8. **ISO Sensitivity Indicator:** Shows when Auto ISO is enabled.
9. **Release Mode:** Shows current release mode.
10. **Memory Card Slot 2:** Shows which card slots are currently selected.

11. Memory Card Slot 1: Shows which card slots are currently selected.

12. AF-Area Mode Indicator: Displays current AF-area mode.

13. Focus Mode: Shows current focus mode.

14. Shooting Menu Bank: Shows which menu bank is currently selected.

03 ESSENTIAL MODES AND SETTINGS

MODE SHOOTING MODES

Press the Mode button and rotate the Main Command Dial to choose the shooting mode.

P (Programmed Auto): Camera sets shutter speed and aperture based on metering info and current ISO.

S (Shutter Priority): You set shutter speed; camera sets aperture based on metering info and current ISO. Shutter speed can be set between 30 sec. and 1/32000 sec.

A (Aperture Priority): You set aperture; camera sets shutter speed based on metering info and current ISO. Range of apertures depends on the lens.

M (Manual): You set both shutter speed and aperture. Can set shutter speed to Bulb or Time modes for long exposures.

METERING MODES

Menu > Photo Shooting Menu > Metering

Matrix: Uses the whole frame along with lens information (color, distance) from G, E, and D lenses to determine exposure. Best for most situations.

Center-Weighted: Uses information predominantly from center of frame to determine exposure.

Spot: Uses area under current focus point to determine exposure.

Highlight-Weighted: Camera determines exposure in order to keep detail in the brightest highlights.

EXPOSURE COMPENSATION

Press Exposure Compensation button on top right of camera and turn Main Command Dial to adjust exposure from –5 (darker) to +5 (lighter) in 1/3-stop increments.

Note: In Manual (M) exposure mode, Exposure Compensation will change exposure indicator but not shutter speed or aperture.

FOCUS MODES

AF-S (Single AF): Focus starts when Shutter Release button is pressed halfway and locks when focus is achieved. Best for stationary subjects.

AF-C (Continuous AF): Focus starts when Shutter Release button is pressed halfway and continues to focus until photo is taken. Best for moving subjects.

AF-F (Full-Time AF): Only available in Movie mode. Focus tracks subject continuously until Shutter Release button is pressed halfway.

M (Manual Focus): Focusing is accomplished by turning focusing ring on lens barrel.

AF-AREA MODES

Pinpoint AF: Offers a very small, precise AF point that is best for static subjects where the focus is critical on a small part of the subject (AF-S only).

Single-Point AF: A slightly larger focus point than Pinpoint, this mode is available in AF-S as well as AF-C. The Single-Point mode uses one of the camera's 493 AF points.

Dynamic-Area AF (Small, Medium, Large): Uses either the small, medium, or large group of focus points, and if the subject leaves the focus area briefly, the camera uses the surrounding AF points to keep focus locked (AF-C only).

Wide-Area AF (Small, Large): Similar to Single-Point AF, except the camera focuses on a wider area.

Wide-Area AF (C1) (C2): Allows the photographer to choose the area (measured in focus points) used for the autofocus.

3D-Tracking: Select initial focus point and the camera will attempt to track the subject across the frame (AF-C in photo mode only).

Subject-Tracking AF: Select initial focus point and the camera will attempt to track the subject across the frame. This is only available in video mode.

Auto-Area AF: Camera automatically detects the subject and decides on the focus area.

RELEASE MODES

Press the Release Mode Dial Lock Release and rotate the Release Mode Dial to the selected mode.

S (Single Frame): Takes a single shot every time Shutter Release button is pressed.

L (Continuous Low): Takes between 1–10 frames per second (FPS) as long as you press Shutter Release button.

H (Continuous High): Takes between 10–20 frames per second (FPS) as long as you press Shutter Release button.
Self-Timer: When Shutter Release button is pressed fully, camera waits a set time before taking photo. To set the delay, press and hold the Release Mode button and turn a Command Dial.
Quick Release-Mode Selection: Used to choose between the High-Speed Frame Capture modes (C30)/(C120): C30 uses 30fps (frames per second), C120 uses 120fps.

WHITE BALANCE

Press and hold the WB button and rotate the Main Command Dial.

The **A (Auto)** setting is best for most situations. White balance can be set to shift colors warmer, cooler, or keep them accurate. Other settings are all matched to different lighting types. For truest colors, pick the type of lighting being used to illuminate scene.

FILE FORMAT / IMAGE QUALITY

Hold the QUAL button and rotate the Main Command Dial to select from the following options.

RAW (NEF): The RAW data from the image sensor is recorded each time a photo is taken.

RAW (NEF) + JPEG: The camera saves two files each time the Shutter Release button is pressed, a RAW file and a JPEG file. You can decide the quality of the JPEG (fine, normal, or basic; options with a star maximize image quality). Only the JPEG is shown during playback. Deleting the JPEG also deletes the RAW file.

JPEG: The camera saves a JPEG file each time the Shutter Release button is pressed. You can decide the quality of the JPEG (fine, normal, or basic; options with a star maximize image quality).

04 OTHER HELPFUL SETTINGS

PICTURE CONTROLS

Hold the Fn4 button and rotate the Main Command Dial to choose the Picture Control.

Allows you to adjust settings for JPEG images. Adjustable settings are Sharpness, Clarity, Saturation, Brightness, and Hue. Eight preset picture controls can all be adjusted: **A (AUTO), SD(Standard), NL (Neutral), VI (Vivid), MC (Monochrome), PT (Portrait), LS (Landscape), FL (Flat),** and the custom option **01–20 (Creative Picture Control)**. You can modify the picture controls in the Manage Picture Control menu, adjusting Effect Level, Sharpness, Contrast, Brightness, Saturation, Hue, Filter Effects, and Toning. Monochrome images can have a Yellow, Orange, Red, or Green filter applied.

ϟ FLASH MODES

Press the Flash button and rotate the Main Command Dial.

Fill Flash: The flash fires with each shot. When using P or A shooting mode, camera uses shutter speed between 1/60–1/200 sec. (1/60–1/8000 sec. when Auto FP High-Speed Sync is selected).

Red-Eye Reduction: Flash fires twice: first pre-flash burst is so that subject's pupils close, reducing the red-eye effect. Not good for moving subjects.

Slow Sync: Flash is used in conjunction with slower shutter speeds to allow ambient light into photo. Only available in P and A shooting modes.

Slow Sync and Red-Eye Reduction: Combines red-eye reduction pre-flash and slow sync for better portraits taken when you want ambient light in photo.

Rear-Curtain Sync: Flash fires at end of exposure, creating more natural-looking light trails if subject is moving.

Flash Off: Flash does not fire.

COLOR SPACE

Photo Shooting Menu > Color Space

sRGB: Smaller color space. Best when images are used directly from camera.

Adobe RGB: Larger color space. Best when images will be edited with post-processing software.

HIGHLIGHT WARNING (BLINKIES)

Playback Menu > Playback Display Options, select Highlight Display

Shows pure-white areas as blinking highlights on playback. Useful to know if areas are being overexposed.

NOISE REDUCTION

Photo Shooting Menu > Long Exposure NR

Reduces noise in images with shutter speeds of 1 second or longer. Doubles time needed to save image to memory card.

Photo Shooting Menu > High ISO NR

Reduces noise in images taken at high ISO settings. Use Normal for default, Low for less noise reduction, and High for more noise reduction. You can also select Off, which still might apply some noise reduction, but it is less than Low.

AUTO ISO

Hold ISO button and rotate Sub-Command Dial to turn Auto ISO on or off.

You can set the **Maximum Sensitivity** (the highest ISO the camera will use) in Photo Shooting Menu > ISO Sensitivity Settings.

DISP BUTTON

Press the DISP button to cycle through up to five customizable displays.

To choose which displays are accessible when you press the DISP button during shooting, go to Menu > Custom Settings Menu > d Shooting / display > d18 [Custom monitor shooting display]. Highlight Display 2 through Display 5 and press OK to select or deselect. The selected displays will be shown when the DISP button is pressed. Display 1 cannot be deselected.

To select what is shown on each display, select Display 1 through 4 (Display 5 is the information display and cannot be customized) and press right on the Multi Selector. Now select what you want to see on the displays.

SIMPLE (Basic shooting info): Shows shooting mode, shutter speed, aperture, and other basic information.

DETAIL (Detailed shooting info): Shows focus mode, AF-area mode, WB, and other detailed information.
Touch Controls: Shows the options that can be accessed by touch, including touch AF and the *i* menu.
Virtual Horizon: Shows a virtual horizon.
Histogram: Displays the RGB histogram.
Framing Grid: Displays a grid that is customizable at Menu > Custom Settings Menu > d Shooting / display > d16 [Grid Type]
Center Indicator: Displays crosshairs at the center of the frame.

You can also set what is shown on the viewfinder when you press the DISP button at Menu > Custom Settings Menu > d Shooting / display > d19 [Custom viewfinder shooting display]. All the choices are the same with the exception of Touch Controls, which are not available.

ACTIVE D-LIGHTING

Photo Shooting Menu > Active D-Lighting

Used to help preserve detail that can be lost in both the darkest and brightest parts of a high-contrast image. You can set the strength to Auto, Extra High 2, Extra High 1, High, Normal, or Low, or you can turn Active D-Lighting off.

Note: This feature can cause image issues such as banding and noise at higher ISO settings.

BKT AUTO BRACKETING

Photo Shooting Menu > Auto Bracketing Set

Auto Bracketing is used to take a set of images where exposure, flash power, white balance, or Active D-Lighting is changed slightly between each frame. You can set the camera to whichever option you would like to bracket.

Exposure (AE) & Flash: Changes the exposure and the flash power.

Exposure (AE): Changes the exposure.

Flash: Changes the flash power.

WB: Changes the white balance.

ADL: Changes the amount of the Active D-Lighting applied.

Hold the BKT button down and rotate the Main Command Dial to choose the number of shots in the bracketing sequence. Then hold the BKT button down and rotate the Sub-Command Dial to set the exposure increment.

For ADL bracketing, you choose the number of shots, and that determines the bracketing sequence.

WIRELESS CONNECTION (SNAPBRIDGE)

Use the Nikon SnapBridge app on your smartphone or tablet to connect the Z9 to the device.

Allows for wireless downloading of images and remote control of camera. You can connect your device to your camera using Bluetooth (which allows for the automatic downloading of images to your device as they're taken) or Wi-Fi.

MULTIPLE EXPOSURES

Create in-camera multiple exposures from 2 to 10 RAW (NEF) files:

1. Select Photo Shooting Menu > Multiple Exposure Mode, and press right on the Multi Selector.
2. Choose the Multiple Exposure mode:
   On (series): Takes multiple exposures until Off is selected.
   On (single photo): Takes one multiple exposure.
   Off: Turns multiple exposures off.
3. Select Number of Shots to combine.
4. Pick the Overlay mode:
   Add: The images are combined without any modification.
   Average: Before the images are combined, the gain for each image is divided by the total number of images to create a proper exposure.
   Lighten: Camera uses only lightest pixels of each image to create an overall light image.
   Darken: Camera uses only darkest pixels of each image to create an overall dark image.

5. Choose whether to keep the individual images by selecting Save Individual Pictures (RAW) and choosing On or Off, then pressing OK.
6. Choose whether to view the progress in the display by selecting Overlay Shooting and choosing On or Off, then pressing OK.
7. To use an existing photo as the first exposure, choose Select First Exposure (RAW), then press right on the Multi Selector. Highlight the image using the Multi Selector and press OK.

Take the selected number of photos and the camera will combine them into a single JPEG image. (If you chose to use an existing photo as the first exposure in step 7, shooting will start with the second exposure.)

HDR HDR

Combine two JPEG images to reduce the contrast and improve tonal range:

1. Select Photo Shooting Menu > HDR Overlay, and press right on the Multi Selector.

2. Choose HDR Mode and press right on the Multi Selector to shoot either a series (On [Series]) or just a single occurrence (On [Single Photo]), or select Off, which stops HDR shooting.
3. Choose the HDR Strength from the following: Auto, Extra High, High, Normal, or Low.
4. Choose whether to keep the individual exposures (Save Individual Pictures [RAW]).
5. Press the Shutter Release button once to take the two photos that end up as a single HDR JPEG.

If the camera is set to Series, it will continue to take HDR images until you open the menu and change that setting to Off. If the camera is set to Single Photo, it will turn HDR off after you take the first HDR photo.

TIME-LAPSE MOVIES

Create a time-lapse movie in-camera:

1. Select Photo Shooting Menu > Time-Lapse Video, and press right on the Multi Selector.
2. Select the Interval, which is the time between each photo. Set in minutes and seconds.
3. Select the Shooting Time, which is how long to shoot (up to 23 hours and 59 minutes).

4. Choose whether you want to use Exposure Smoothing. When On, the camera automatically tries to smooth any big changes in the exposure.
5. Choose the Image Area to capture (FX for full frame or DX for cropped sensor).
6. Choose the Video File Type: H.265 8-Bit (MOV) or H.264 8-Bit (MP4).
7. Choose the Frame Size/Frame Rate.
8. Turn Interval Priority On or Off. On ensures that frames shot in P or A mode will use the set interval even if that creates an underexposed image.
9. Select whether the camera needs to Focus Before Each Shot.
10. Select a Destination, or which card slot to save the time-lapse to.
11. Select Start and press OK.

INTVL INTERVAL TIMER PHOTOGRAPHY

Set the camera to take a series of photos over a period of time:

1. Select Photo Shooting Menu > Interval Timer Shooting, and press right on the Multi Selector.

2. Set Start options to begin either Now or at least 1 minute in future (Choose Day/Time).

3. Set the Interval between photos (Hours/Minutes/Seconds).

4. Set number of intervals and the number of shots per interval (Intervals x Shots/Interval).

5. Turn Exposure Smoothing On or Off.

6. Turn Interval Priority On or Off. When On, photos shot in P or A mode will be taken at the chosen interval; when Off, the camera will use shutter speed to achieve proper exposure even if that is longer than the selected interval.

7. Choose whether the camera should Focus Before Each Shot.

8. Choose Options to set whether the camera combines interval-timer shooting with AE Bracketing (set the number of shots and the change in exposure [increment]) or Time-Lapse Video (choose the settings for Video File Type, Frame Size/ Frame Rate, and Destination). Or set to Off.

9. Select Starting Storage Folder to choose whether a new folder is created for each new sequence, and whether image numbering is reset when a new folder is created.

10. Select Start and press OK.

06 TYPICAL SHOOTING SCENARIOS

SHOOTING SCENARIO
PORTRAIT

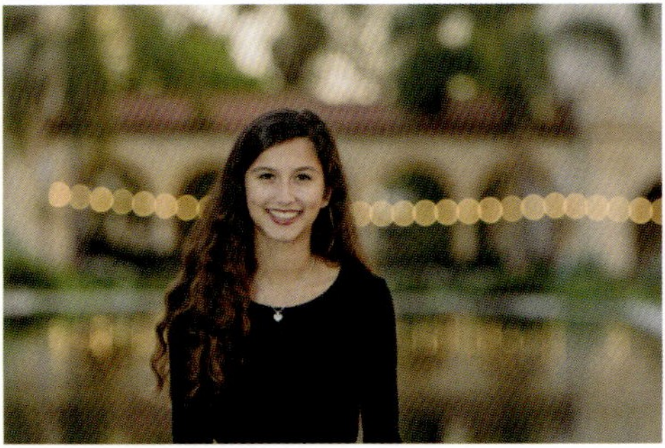

KEY PRINCIPLES

- The key to a portrait like this is shallow depth of field. So shoot in **APERTURE PRIORITY** mode and start with the lowest aperture your lens offers (such as **f/2.8 or f/4**).
- Remember to **focus on the eyes**.
- If the image is too dark or too light, use **EXPOSURE COMPENSATION** to adjust the brightness level.

- If the image is blurry from a slow shutter speed, **raise the ISO** to increase your sensor's sensitivity to light, thus allowing for a faster shutter speed.
- Remember to use a **focal length of 50mm or greater** so that you don't distort your subject's face.

SHOOTING SCENARIO
GROUP PORTRAIT

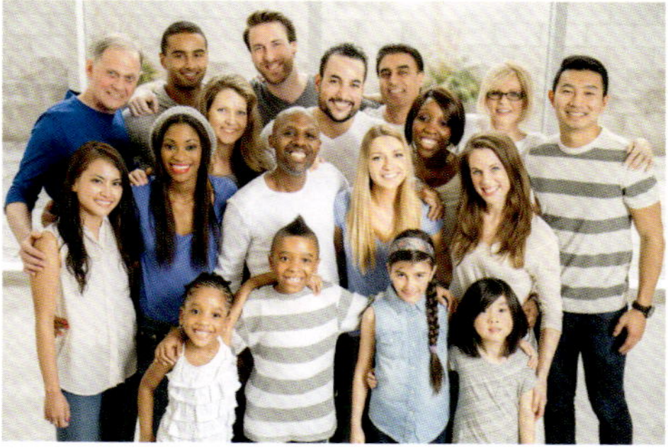

KEY PRINCIPLES

- To get everyone in focus, you need a deep depth of field. So shoot in **APERTURE PRIORITY** mode and set the aperture between **f/8–f/16**.

- **Focus on the person in the middle of the group**. Check focus by using the Zoom In button to view it at 100% and check faces in the front and back rows. If anyone is out of focus, use a smaller aperture for deeper depth of field.
- Use **MATRIX METERING** to account for the light in the entire scene.
- **Arrange the group so they can all see you** (and you can see them).
- Use **EXPOSURE COMPENSATION** if the image is too bright or too dark.
- If image is blurry, **raise the ISO** to allow the camera to use a faster shutter speed.

SHOOTING SCENARIO

LANDSCAPE

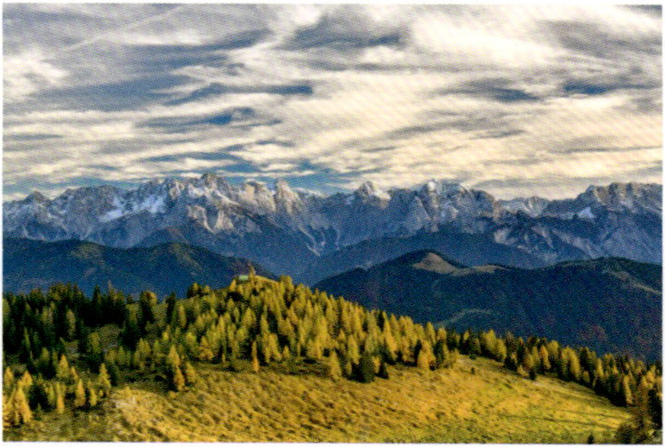

KEY PRINCIPLES

- Shoot in **APERTURE PRIORITY** to control depth of field, and start with **f/16** to ensure deep depth of field.
- **Use a tripod** to eliminate camera movement. Whenever your camera is on a tripod, also make sure that **VIBRATION REDUCTION is turned off**.
- Use **MATRIX METERING** mode and **SINGLE AUTOFOCUS (AF-S)** Focus mode.
- **Set the ISO to a low setting (64–200)** to avoid any digital noise.

- Shoot in **RAW** so that you have the most available information when editing later.
- Consider **BRACKETING** your exposures.

SHOOTING SCENARIO
FREEZE ACTION

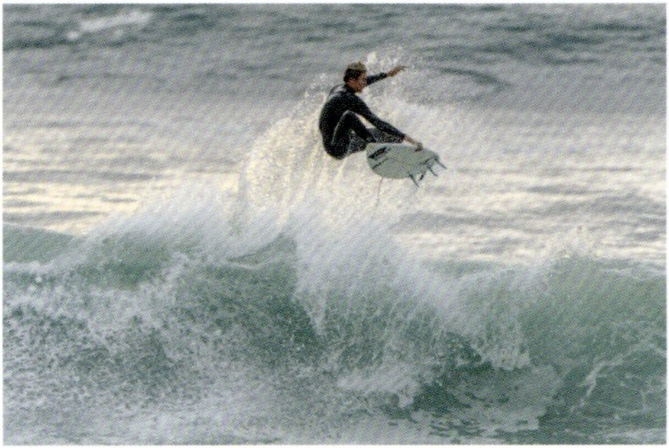

KEY PRINCIPLES

- Use **SHUTTER PRIORITY** mode and set the shutter speed to a value that will freeze the action. The appropriate shutter speed depends on your subject and its movement, but could be anywhere between **1/500–1/32000 sec**.

- Use **CONTINUOUS AUTOFOCUS (AF-C)** so that the camera keeps focusing as the subject moves.
- If the image is dark or blurry, **raise the ISO** or try AUTO ISO to automatically have the camera adjust the ISO as needed.

SHOOTING SCENARIO
SHOWING MOTION—PANNING

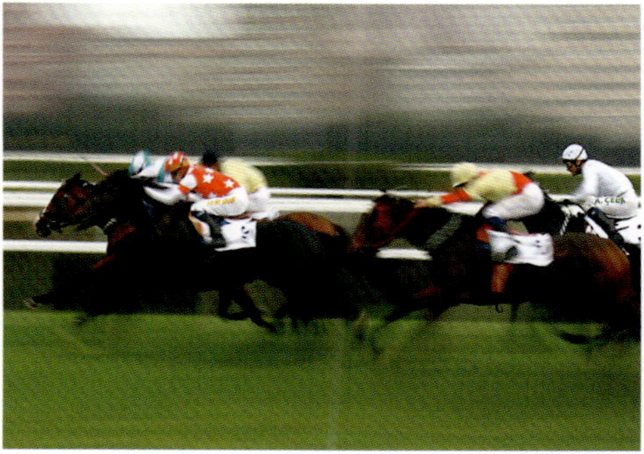

KEY PRINCIPLES

- Shoot in **SHUTTER PRIORITY** mode and use a slow-enough shutter speed to allow for the subject to move during the exposure.

- **Follow the subject** across the frame as you shoot.
- Try using **LIVE VIEW**, which allows you to see the subject during the exposure.
- Use **CONTINUOUS AUTOFOCUS (AF-C)**, and 3D-Tracking AF to help keep the subject in focus.

SHOOTING SCENARIO
LOW-LIGHT ACTION

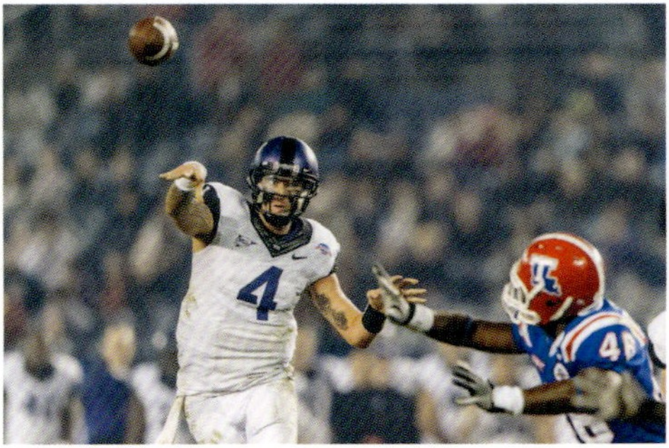

KEY PRINCIPLES

- Shoot in **APERTURE PRIORITY** mode and use a wide aperture such as **f/2.8 or f/4**.
- Use **SPOT METERING** and meter on the subject's face.

- Use **CONTINUOUS AUTOFOCUS (AF-C)** and a single AF point.
- **Set the ISO to 1600 or higher**, depending on the amount of available light.
- If the image is blurry, **increase the ISO** to allow for a faster shutter speed.

SHOOTING SCENARIO
LONG EXPOSURE

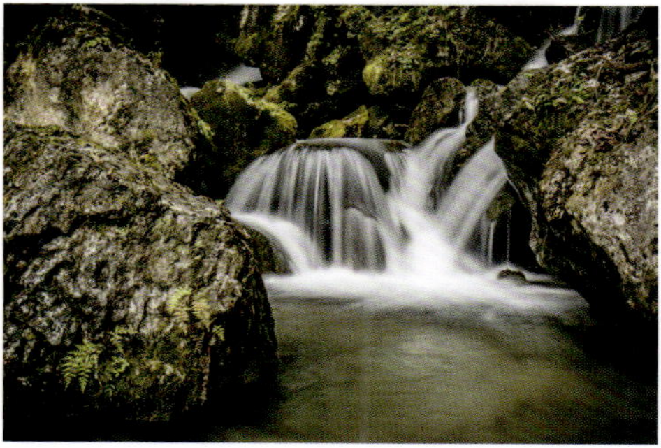

KEY PRINCIPLES

- Use **MANUAL** shooting mode, which allows you to use the **BULB** or **TIME** setting for long exposures.

- **Use a tripod** to keep the camera stable. **Turn off any VIBRATION REDUCTION feature**.
- Use the **SINGLE AUTOFOCUS (AF-S)** Focus mode, or try manual focus if the camera is having a hard time locking on focus.
- **Use a low ISO (64–400)** and **shoot RAW** to ensure a high-quality file.
- **Use a remote** with a lock to avoid touching (shaking) the camera.